CELEBRATION:
CHRISTMAS IN NEW YORK

For Jay

CONTENTS

ACKNOWLEDGEMENTS

One cannot begin to thank anyone without first acknowledging the enormous debt of gratitude due Meg Crane and Ira Sturtevant of Ponzi & Weill, not only for their support but for their expertise in graphic design and editing which was crucial to this book.

A personal thank you to John Taylor for his handsome introduction.

Special thanks to the photographers Edward North and Alan Batt for providing the visual material in this book.

Thanks to the publisher Allen D. Bragdon for his many considerations.

A big thank you to my associates and staff, Jay Spectre, Inc. for their support.

This book could not have been realized without the very generous cooperation of the celebrities and personalities who allowed us into their Christmas Celebrations: to them the author extends his warmest thanks.

For their generous assistance and support: Robert Woolley and his celebrity rolodex, John Loring, Tiffany & Co., Mark Gilbertson, and Renny Reynolds, Dorothy Melvin and Heather Mazzio. many thanks.

In addition: The Office of Mayor Dinkins, Julia Hansen, Leila Heller, Nathalie Thomas, William Starrett, Leonard Finger, Baroness for Suzanne Bartsch, Mary Van Pendl, Scott George, David Howard's Studio, Carole Lembo, Nohra Haime, Josephine Sophian, Bob Crane, Bermuda Limousine Co., Arty Nichols Carriage Service, The K-9 Club, The Public Relations and Special Events Departments of Radio City Music Hall®, Rockefeller Center, Metropolitan Museum of Art, Macy's, Barney's, Saks Fifth Avenue, Henri Bendel, James II Galleries, Ltd., Homma-Lipton, St. Thomas Church, The Cathedral of St. John the Divine. The restaurants: Cafe des Artistes, Alo Alo, Harry Cipriani, Mortimer's, The Russian Tea Room, Cafe Tabac, Doubles, 21 Club.

Thanks to the additional photographers: Joan Vitale Strong, Robin Bowman, Dennis Golub, Steven Caras, David Sahadi, John Simon, Bachrach Studios. Paul Hyman, Martha Andersen, Colin Sharp.

Knowing that many individuals and companies have been left out, a blanket thank you is extended to these people.

G.N.B.

A CELEBRATION OF NEW YORK!

My move to New York from South Africa in September 1977 was the culmination of a love affair with the city which began as a visiting teenager.

Today, it is my home. I enjoy an apartment that is 99 blocks from the spot where George Washington took the oath of office as President of the United States, 54 blocks from the Great Hall of Cooper Union where Abraham Lincoln delivered the Emancipation Proclamation, 42 blocks from Teddy Roosevelt's home, and 5 blocks from Franklin Roosevelt's.

I can walk to Egypt's Temple of Dendur, see two Gutenberg Bibles in J. P. Morgan's library, take a bus to a medieval chapel, a boat to the Statue of Liberty, and visit a different art gallery or museum every day of the year without seeing them all.

I can dance to any tune, eat in any language, worship as I wish, and study just about any subject known to the world in any of the city's dozens and dozens of colleges, universities, and institutes. On any given day, I have my choice of forty or fifty different stage productions and hundreds of movies. Every one of the world's major orchestras, dance companies, divas, and virtuosos will visit my city. And every one of the world's most gifted, most important, and best loved people either lives here or will pass through the city.

New York is the liveliest, most creative, most inspiring city in the world. And for me it has been the warmest, friendliest place I have ever been.

This wonderful city has been visited by a plague called AIDS. And the city has responded as only New York can. This book is my response. It is a Celebration of New York City at Christmas time, the warmest, most wonderful time of the year. It is dedicated to the memory of Jay Spectre, my business partner and friend, and to the memory of all the other New Yorkers who have been affected by AIDS. It is dedicated, as well, to all those people who have contributed and are contributing so much to ease the life of AIDS patients and to fund AIDS research. Proceeds from the sale of this book will be donated to DIFFA (Design Industry Foundation for AIDS) in support of AIDS research.

Geoffrey N. Bradfield

New York's venerable Mayor Dinkins, at the City Hall
Christmas Tree Lighting surrounded by youth of Manhattan.

INTRODUCTION

The design world has been devastated by the AIDS plague, and those who are part of it must struggle at times to resist being overwhelmed by a sense of loss. Life, in such bleak moments, needs to be resoundingly affirmed. For this reason Geoffrey Bradfield, partner of the late Jay Spectre, decided to devote himself to this pictorial exploration of the world's most magnetic city (and uncontested design center) during its most exhilarating (and decorative) holiday. His hope was that the book would celebrate life and, in addition, help save lives; all sales proceeds will be donated to the Design Industry Foundation for AIDS.

Christmas throughout the world is largely a private affair. In this book, Geoffrey wanted to capture the gloriously public way it is celebrated here. He took the position that New York's Christmas season actually begins on Thanksgiving Day, when Santa Claus arrives in town courtesy of his float in the Macy's parade, and ends with another public celebration, the Twelfth Night festivities at the Cathedral of St. John the Divine. The photographs, most of them by Alan Batt and Edward North, were all taken during the 1992 Christmas season.

It is all here, from the origami tree at the American Museum of Natural History to the snowswept glow of the Empire State Building to Liz Smith and her cowboy boots in front of the tree at Rockefeller Center. (When celebrities whom Geoffrey approached learned the purpose of the book, they all volunteered their time with enthusiasm.) "Celebration: Christmas in New York" is by turns romantic, spectacular, touching, and wry. And it is, as Geoffrey hoped, a resounding affirmation of life in New York.

John Taylor
Author of *Circus of Ambition*

Santa's Sleigh

The entire audience is happily transported when Santa appears in his sleigh, one of the highpoints of Radio City Music Hall®'s Christmas Special.

9 West 57 Street wears huge red and green candy canes illuminated by a myriad of sparkling points of light.

※

Two Metropolitan Angels

An exquisite rococo angel, possibly fashioned by Giuseppe Sammartino over two hundred years ago, swings a censer over the Metropolitan Museum of Art's famous creche.

Socialite Blaine Trump, a leading angel with "God's Love We Deliver," puts the finishing touches to one of the Christmas baskets she'll deliver to homebound AIDS patients on Christmas Day.

Paper Perfect

Deftly folded by hand, hundreds of origami figures surround this truly unique holiday tree with an oriental aura at New York's famed American Museum of Natural History.

Picture Perfect

Manhattan's most visible young couple, scion of the Fairchild family, sociable James and stunning Whitney St. John.

✳
Modern

High style fashion designer Mary MacFadden, in her showroom, creates an exquisite minimalist tree of grapevine topped by a Christmas angel.

❄ Christmas Traditions

The Neapolitan creche at the Metropolitan Museum of Art consists of nearly 200 figures embracing the exquisitely sculpted Holy Family with angels and shepherds, the Magi with Orientals and Moors, and country and townsfolk, portrayed with exhilarating realism.

A joyous Christmas party at the home of the Peabodys (Judy, Sam, and daughter Elizabeth), one of the first families to join the fight against AIDS.

Party Day

What a cool way to celebrate the holidays:
a figure eight on Wollman rink surrounded by
snowy fields in the midst of the city.

❄
Party Night

Susan Williamson, Bill Beutel, Jamee Gregory, and
Mark Gilbertson — with Santa on skates — take time out
from the Annual Christmas Party Jamee hosts at the
Wollman Rink for all the people who helped the Central Park
Conservancy throughout the year.

❄
New Hat

Dashing Eric Javits crowns
talk show queen
Sally Jessy Raphael with one
of his ultra chic chapeaux.

Old Hat

A Nutcracker from
Rockefeller Center's Skating Rink
looks on in envy.

Dashing through the Snow

A twilight visit to Victorian days in one of Central
Park's famous horse-drawn carriages.

❄

Dashing in the Snow
Super star fashion designer
Donna Karan takes a dreamy
stroll through the snowdrifts
in Central Park.

❋ Before

Sotheby's Robert Woolley, Society's Favorite Auctioneer, rests up at home before a hectic holiday schedule visiting parents and parties and doing a charity auction for Oscar de la Renta's orphanage, Casa de Mer.

❋ After

For publishing magnate Tim Forbes and his wife Ann, family tradition runs deep, hosting their annual Christmas Party in their traditional Victorian townhouse.

✳
Christmas Fun

Genial and amusing interior designer
Mario Buatta enters into the spirit
of yuletide jollity while shopping
at the James II Galleries. For him, the
holiday season in New York is
reminiscent of Dickensian Christmases
he read of as a child.

Christmas Fantasy

Henri Bendel's fabulous Fifth Avenue window presents an ultra chic combination of faux jewelry with genuine greenery.

High Creativity

A tree of Christmas baskets filled with holiday glitter greets shoppers as they enter Henri Bendel's stunning Fifth Avenue store.

✳ High Profile

Elegant and charming
international designer
Oscar de la Renta with
a model sporting his
romantic creation
for the female Santa.

❋
Come for a Ride

Romance through the Park with effervescent
actress, singer Jane Powell.

Come for a Stay

Shining across snowswept
Grand Army Plaza, the brilliantly lit
entrance of The Plaza Hotel
invites you for tea in the Palm Court,
dinner in the Oak Room,
or a weekend in one of its
luxurious suites.

※
Dessert Troika

President of the Drama League
Julia Hansen with charismatic director,
choreographer, dancer Tommy Tune
and the Russian Tea Room's
Faith Stewart Gordon at the
Russian Tea Room, located just
a little to the left of Carnegie Hall.

Desert Troika

The Three Wise Men's Camels prepare to enter
Radio City Music Hall® for their cameo appearance
in the Christmas pageant.

Family Gathering

Arbiter of taste, gracious southerner Betty Sherrill, President of McMillen Inc., at a Christmas get-together with her grandchildren in her Sutton Place apartment.

Family Attraction

One of the happiest outings of the holiday season, generation after generation of New York parents have accompanied their wide-eyed children to The Nutcracker, a brilliant marriage of Tchaikovsky's magical score and Balanchine's inspired choreography.

Magic and Romance

The New York City Ballet's quintessential presentation of The Nutcracker: the dancers, the music, the scenery conspire to weave a magical moment while principal dancers Heather Watts and Jock Soto create a romantic one.

❄ Art at Home

The toast of Paris, international sculptor Fernando Botero and his wife sculptress Sophia Vari spend Christmas at home in their East Side apartment.

Home of Art

The Metropolitan Museum, here dusted with snow, is one of the city's stellar attractions, and host each year to more fans than Yankee Stadium.

Artiste

Barney's pays holiday homage to Madonna
in one of a series of sophisticated celebrity windows
by Simon Doonan

Artist

Enfant terrible of the art world,
Jeff Koons strikes a provocative pose,
life imitating art, with oversized Christmas
flowers in his pristine studio.

In the lion's den, the celebrated Dominick Dunne savors the success of yet another stellar best seller *A Season in Purgatory*.

❋

Literary Lions

Standing guard over The New York Public Library's venerable collection of more than thirty million books, manuscripts, microfilms, maps, recordings, photographs, sheets of music, and much, much more.

Architectural Digest's Editor in Chief Paige Rense Christmas shops for her favorite friends at Robert Homma, William Lipton's fantasy shop.

Walking in the Park

A parade of New York's best friends take the trusted pros of the K-9 Club for a walk.

❋
Sitting by the fire

Bobby Short,
King of the Carlyle,
relaxes with his
best friend, Chili
in their East
Side apartment.

Reason for Revelry

Christmas brings together (left to right) Douglas P. Braff,
Meg Williams, Gigi Mortimer, Jennifer Creel, and John B. Niven
for holiday drinks at Mortimer's, a favorite uptown East Side
Watering Hole.

Two Reasons for Revelry

With birthday and Christmas in close proximity, Crystal Moffet Perry (standing) celebrates both with friends (left to right) Nina Tower, Ariane Noel, Helen Schifter, Laura Blodgett, and Lillian Wang in an all-dressed-in-leather party at the Cafe Tabac, a favorite downtown East Side Watering Hole.

❋
West Side Elegance

Dressed courtyard at the Apthorpe,
a Broadway classic.

East Side Elegance

Chappie Morris holds court for
Marina Elser, Debbie Bancroft, Sue Chalom,
Joy Diaz de Rivera, and Muffy Potter
at Sue Chalom's Park Avenue apartment.

✽
At the Table

Kevin McKenzie, Director of the American Ballet
Theatre, and Martine van Hamel, former Prima
Ballerina with the company, offer a toast
at famed Harry Cipriani's.

✽
At the Barre

Trans-Atlantic couple together in
David Howard's studio: London racing car
designer Christopher with his wife,
New York's Cynthia Harvey, a principal
dancer at the American Ballet Theatre.

The Rites of Winter

One of Society's oldest seasonal observances: "Coming out" at The Debutante Cotillion and Christmas Ball, held each year at New York's fabled Hotel Waldorf-Astoria for the benefit of The New York Infirmary-Beekman Downtown Hospital.

❄

The Debutante Committee for the 1992 Cotillion comprised (left to right, front row first): the Misses Lina Russell Harman, Katherine Elizabeth Christopherson, Brooke Edmunds Brodsky, Sarah Pearce Murphy, and Co- Chairmen Cornelia Mai Erckenlentz and Joanne Gallagher Lembo.

Vision of the Past

Using the past as his palette, Simon Doonan composes an eclectic interior for one of his captivating Barney's windows.

❉ Vision of Today

Spanish Institute Junior Chairman and daughter of Count and Countess de la Maza, Victoria Hempel in her Beekman Place apartment.

✳
Packages, Packages, Packages

Doyenne of fashion Pauline Trigére brings hers home to her Park Avenue apartment in a Bermuda limousine.

Packages, Packages, Packages

Robin Roberts, of Clarence House, loads up his black Turbo Bentley before heading to Twin Ponds, his country estate.

Famous Scene

The 21 Club, since Prohibition days, New York City's No. 1 gathering place for the rich and famous.

Famous Author

Best-selling Barbara Taylor Bradford, and her writing companion Bichon Frise "Gemmy", sets a romantic Christmas table in her Sutton Place dining room.

✳ Christmas Present

At home among the grandeur of Old Masters,
Jocelyn Kress in her townhouse, with sons
Zachary and Jedediah Turner.

Christmas Past

An evocative combination of Christmas ornaments
from long ago in a chic Chelsea antique shop.

Trees and Lights

explode the night on
New York's Park Avenue.

❄

Ribbons and Bows

trim a ten-foot tree for international
hostess Jacqueline Blanchard Peralta-Ramos
and her trio of devoted schnauzers.

John Loring

Tiffany's Senior Vice President of Design
enjoys a replica of the parlor from
Mimi Sheraton's authentic New York townhouse,
part of Tiffany's spectacular Christmas display.

Eleanor Lambert

Legendary style setter of the fashion world
hangs the mistletoe and prepares a Christmas party
for a few close friends at home.

❄
Gala at the Dyson's
Vivacious hostess June Dyson
in her Park Avenue apartment
prepares to meet their guests at
her Christmas party for the
American Ballet Theatre.

❄
Picnic at Tiffany's
Brooke Hayward, accomplished daughter
of Leland Hayward and Margaret Sullavan and wife
of Peter Duchin, creates a fantasy picnic
of whimsical forest creatures in the snow for her
Christmas display at Tiffany's

Santa's Coming!

Thanksgiving eve and Santa's golden sleigh and prancing reindeer are ready to carry St. Nick down Broadway, as New York's Christmas season officially starts with Macy's Thanksgiving Day Parade.

❄

Santa's Been Here!

Christmas morning and Santa's presents wait under the tree for television's high profile Deborah Norville, husband Karl Wellner, and son Niki.

✻
Fifth & 57th
Toasting the season, cosmetic whiz
Gayle Hayman and husband
Dr. William Hazeltine, one of the leading
researchers in America's fight against AIDS.

57th & Fifth
Gala lights and a festive snowflake
across from the Hazeltines' window
anchor the very heart
of New York's shopping axis.

Home Port

Once the first sight greeting luxury liners from Europe, today the Ambrose Light Ship celebrates Christmas with a jaunty tree at New York's South Street Seaport.

❄

Home Body

Party magician and planner of the grandest of Christmas events (The Costume Institute Ball at the Metropolitan Museum of Art, being one), John Funt's personal Christmas recipe is simple: an intimate supper at home with good friends.

Neon Tree

Gordon Samrah, Associate Designer with Jay Spectre, Inc., in his Park Avenue South apartment with friend Kei Takada and his new wave Christmas tree.

❄
Neon Lady

New wave Queen of the Night, Suzanne Bartsch, the Christmas Angel who has raised millions for AIDS research.

✳
Christmas Downtown

Innovative fashion designer Jeffrey Banks
in his Chelsea loft with Christmas tree,
hobby horse, and tartan accents.

Historic Washington Square Arch frames the
Greenwich Village Christmas tree with the World
Trade Center in the background.

❄
Garlands of Jewels

Stylish jewelry designed Maria Snyder
(who needs no adornment) and
her brother Simon show off some
of her stunning collection of
holiday bibelots.

Garlands of Light

Drawn by the abundance of lights, fleets of taxis swarm around
Macy's, the world's largest store, helping holiday shoppers
carry their Christmas presents home.

✳
Childhood Toys

Men about town Bobby Browne, Chad Leat, Nick Poshkus, Alan Rogers, and Robert Woolley bear gifts for children to the "Toys for Tots" benefit they co-chair at the Children's Museum of Manhattan.

Childhood Dreams

"Twas the night before Christmas…"

Seasonably Cool

Mr. & Mrs. Snowpersons, along with snowchild, snowdogs, snowtree, and a fireless fireplace extend the coolest of greetings in Barney's witty window by Simon Doonan.

❄
Great Entertainers

The discreet tree in the corner, the Rosenquist on the wall, the yellow, gold, magenta accents, and the garlands of Christmas greenery invite you to enter the living room at Lucy and Phil Suarez's Christmas party in their wondrous Lower East Side apartment. Their more public — and equally welcoming — spaces include, among others, the highly successful restaurants Jo Jo's and Vong.

Towering Trees

Giant palms ablaze with Christmas lights provide a romantic setting for a Japanese couple who traveled over six thousand miles to be married in the World Financial Center's Palm Garden.

❄
Green Sprig

In his loft space downtown, Andre Balazs, hotelier and entrepreneur extrordinaire, harps on Christmas.

❄ **Say Christmas with Flowers**

Nobody, but nobody could imagine Christmas
in New York without tastemaker Renny Reynolds
to set the tone and bring the flowers for the
city's most fabulous holiday fetes.

Say Christmas with a Wreath

Baskets of plenty form an astonishing,
rich wreath suspended over the basket tree
just inside the Fifth Avenue entrance
to Henri Bendel's splendid establishment.

117

❄
Christmas Cheers

Officiating at the hanging of the office Christmas wreath:
Newsweeks' Susan Jacobs and her Advertising Sales
Associates in the Newsweek Building.

Christmas Times

First the presents, then the paper: here it's The New York
Times whose good works include raising money for New
York's Neediest during the holiday season.

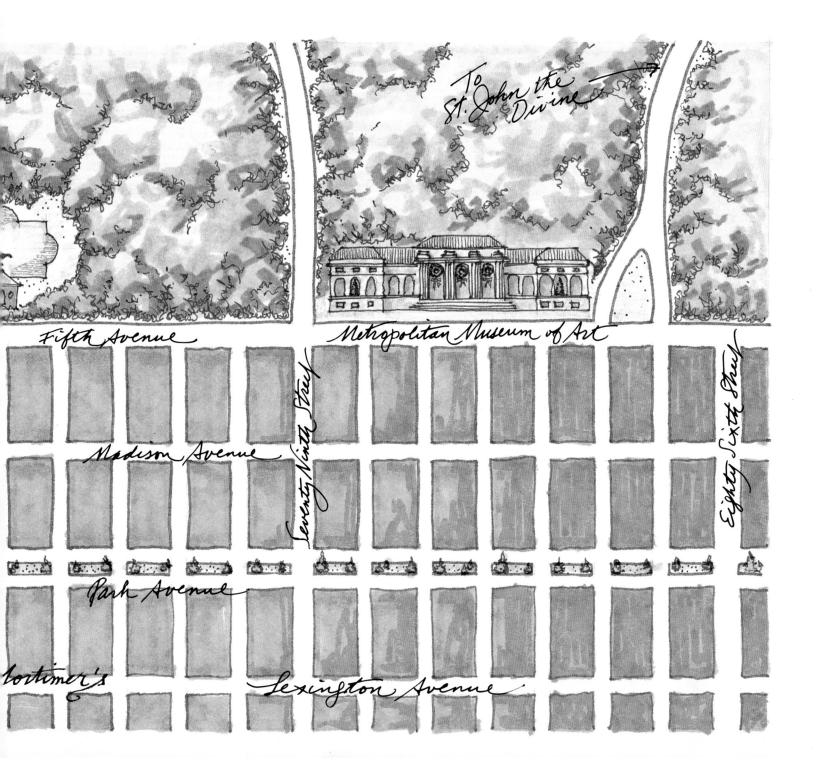

To St. John the Divine →

Fifth Avenue

Metropolitan Museum of Art

Seventy Ninth Street

Eighty Sixth Street

Madison Avenue

Park Avenue

Mortimer's

Lexington Avenue